America's Game
Chicago Cubs

CHRIS W. SEHNERT

ABDO & Daughters
PUBLISHING

Published by Abdo & Daughters, 4940 Viking Dr., Suite 622, Edina, MN 55435.

Cover photo: Allsport
Interior photos: Archive Photos, page 5
Wide World Photo: pages 9-13, 15, 17, 21, 22, 24-28

Edited by Paul Joseph

Library of Congress Cataloging–in–Publication Data

Sehnert, Chris W.
    Chicago Cubs / Chris W. Sehnert
        p. cm. — (America's game)
    Includes index.
    Summary: Focuses on key players and events in the history of the Chicago Cubs, who have represented their city longer than any other professional baseball team.
    ISBN 1-56239-661-7
    1. Chicago Cubs (Baseball team)—Juvenile literature.
[1. Chicago Cubs (Baseball team) 2. Baseball—History.] I. Title.
II. Series.
GV875.C6S45 1996
796.357'64'0977311—dc20   96-5577
                                                            CIP
                                                            AC

Contents

The Chicago Cubs

Baseball is a tradition passed down through generations. Chicago's first professional team was formed in 1870. The same organization remains more than 125 years later!

The Cubs' legacy has endured from the days when Albert Spalding's underhand pitching style ruled baseball in the nineteenth century, to the equally commanding pitcher Greg Maddux of the 1990's.

Hall of Fame players like Mordecai Brown, Ernie Banks and Ferguson Jenkins have all played in the friendly confines of Chicago's Wrigley Field. Chicago baseball fans have witnessed baseball history many times over.

Mark Grace, Sammy Sosa, and Ryne Sandberg hold the future for a team whose last World Championship came in 1908.

The Chicago Cubs have represented their city longer than any other professional baseball team. They pioneered Major League Baseball. Their historical tradition carries on today.

Facing page: Chicago Cubs' Sammy Sosa slams a two-run homer against the Colorado Rockies July 20, 1994. The Cubs won 10-9.

White Stockings

The original Cubs were called the Chicago White Stockings. They were the second baseball club to declare themselves professional. The following season in 1871, the White Stockings became founding members of the National Association (NA), baseball's first major league.

The Great Chicago Fire destroyed the White Stockings' ballpark, along with their uniforms and business records, late in the 1871 season. They completed their schedule finishing a close second behind the Philadelphia Athletics. The fire's devastation forced them to drop out of the league for the next two seasons.

The Chicago ballclub returned in 1874, and suffered through two losing seasons. Team President William A. Hulbert was becoming increasingly frustrated with the NA and its lack of organized leadership.

Hulbert gathered the club owners after the 1875 season, and led the way for the formation of the National League (NL). This new and stronger league began play in 1876. It remains the "Senior Circuit" of Major League Baseball to this day.

A.G. Spalding

The White Stockings signed several star players before the NL's inaugural season. Included among these players was Al Spalding.

Spalding was the NA's best pitcher. He led the former league in wins for five straight years, and helped the Boston Red Stockings to four NA Pennants in a row. He was from Illinois, where he returned to become a player-manager for the White Stockings.

Spalding led the NL with 47 wins and finished second with 8 shutouts in 1876. Behind him, the White Stockings won the very first NL Pennant.

Spalding's playing career ended in 1878. At the age of 28, he had won 253 professional games, while losing only 65. His career as a businessman was just beginning.

A. G. Spalding & Bros. Company was formed in 1877 to manufacture and sell sporting goods. His new business became the exclusive provider of the official baseball for the NL. Spalding's Official Baseball Guide was printed annually.

In 1882, Spalding became president of the Chicago White Stockings. He remained an influential character of the game until his death in 1915. Albert Goodwill Spalding was inducted into the Baseball Hall of Fame in 1939.

Cap

Adrian Anson was another of the players signed by William Hulbert before the 1876 season. When Spalding retired in 1878, Anson took over as player-manager of the White Stockings. His role as team leader earned him the nickname "Cap," short for Captain.

Anson led the NL in runs batted in (RBIs) eight times in his career. He won two NL batting crowns, and was the first player in major league history to record 3,000 hits.

The White Stockings won the NL Pennant five more times (1880-82, 1885-86) with Cap at the helm. In the last two, they faced the St. Louis Brown Stockings in an early version of the World Series.

The Brown Stockings were champions of the rival American Association (AA) in those years. The 1885 series finished in a tie (3-3-1), with one game being called because of darkness. In 1886, St. Louis defeated the White Stockings (4-2).

The World Series loss ended Chicago's reign as an NL power. Soon, Anson was the only player left from the pennant-winning years. His new nickname became "Pops." The team changed its name to the Chicago Colts to reflect the youth movement.

After 27 seasons in the "big leagues," Cap Anson played his last game in 1897. It remains the longest major league playing career in history. With "Pops" gone, the ballclub was renamed the Chicago Orphans.

Facing page: Famed first baseman Adrian "Cap" Anson played 27 seasons in the "big leagues."

The Cubs

Chicago's NL ballclub changed its name one last time in 1902, and became the Chicago Cubs. By the end of the "Modern Era's" first decade, the club was back on top of the league's standings.

The Cubs were led by three infielders. Shortstop Joe Tinker, second baseman Johnny Evers, and first baseman Frank Chance headed a defensive lineup that led the NL in fielding average from 1905 to 1908. Beginning in 1906, the Cubs won the NL Pennant four times in five years.

Taking advantage of the Cubs' superior defense was a pitching staff led by Mordecai "Three Finger" Brown. As a seven-year-old Indiana farmboy, Brown accidentally put his right hand into his uncle's corn grinder. His index finger was amputated below the knuckle. Weeks later, he fell while chasing a hog and crushed the third and fourth fingers on the same hand.

Left: Cubs' first baseman Frank Chance.
Facing page: Second baseman Johnny Evers.

The severely disfigured hand of Mordecai Brown provided one of the most wicked curve-balls in baseball history. He won 20 or more games for the Cubs every year from 1906 to 1911. His lifetime earned run average (ERA) of 2.06 ranks third on the all-time list.

In 1906, the Cubs set an all-time record for wins in a season with 116. They finished 20 games in front of the second place New York Giants.

The 1906 World Series featured a crosstown rivalry. Chicago's White Sox won the American League (AL) Pennant. Despite having the lowest team batting average in the majors, they defeated the seemingly invincible Cubs in six games.

The Cubs won another NL Pennant in 1907. In the World Series, Chicago's pitching shut down the Detroit Tigers, allowing only four earned runs in five games. The Chicago Cubs were World Champions for the first time!

Left: Pitching star Mordecai "Three Finger" Brown.
Facing page: Shortstop Joe Tinker.

Bonehead!

The NL pennant race of 1908 was one of the closest ever. Late in the season, the Chicago Cubs, New York Giants, and Pittsburgh Pirates were locked in a struggle atop the NL standings. The season hinged on a single play known as "Merkle's Boner."

In a game at New York's Polo Grounds, the Giants scored what looked like the winning run, on a two-out single in the bottom of the ninth inning.

The Giants' Fred Merkle was on first base when the infamous run crossed the plate. Thinking the game was over, Merkle left the field without advancing to second base. While all of New York celebrated, Cubs second baseman Johnny Evers retrieved the ball and stepped on second base. The umpire called Merkle out, and the run was negated.

Confused Giants fans were ready to tear down the stadium. The game was ruled a tie because of darkness. Two weeks later the Giants and Cubs ended the season with identical records. The Cubs defeated the Giants in a one game playoff to win their third straight NL Pennant!

The Cubs repeated their World Series performance of 1907 by defeating the Detroit Tigers in five games. It was their second straight World Championship, and to date it was their last.

In 1910, the Cubs were NL Champions again. They lost the World Series to the AL's new powerhouse, the Philadelphia Athletics.

By the beginning of the 1914 season, Joe Tinker, Johnny Evers, Frank Chance, and Mordecai Brown had gone on to finish their careers with other teams. All four were later inducted into the Baseball Hall of Fame.

Friendly Confines

In 1916, the Cubs got a new home. North Side Ball Park was built in 1914 to house the Chicago Whales of the Federal League. That league lasted only two years as baseball's third major league, and was defunct after the 1915 season.

The owner of the Whales was Charles Weeghman. When the Federal League went under, he bought the Chicago Cubs. North Side Ball Park then became Cubs' Park.

In 1927, the park took on the name of chewing gum magnate William Wrigley, Jr., who returned the club to glory. It became the last ballpark to put up lights (1988) for night baseball.

To fans of the Cubs it is known as the "Friendly Confines." There is no place in the world quite like the corner of Clark and Addison Streets in Chicago. It's the home of the Cubbies, Wrigley Field!

Wrigley Field, during the 1938 World Series.

15

Hippo

The Cubs finished in the bottom half of the NL Standings the first two years in their new ballpark. They returned to win the NL Pennant in the war-shortened season of 1918.

The pitching staff was led by a 6-foot, 4-inch left-hander nicknamed "Hippo" for his large stature. James "Hippo" Vaughn won a pitching Triple Crown in 1918, with 22 wins, 148 strikeouts, and a 1.74 ERA.

The Boston Red Sox won the AL Pennant in 1918 and were too tough for the Cubs. In close-scoring pitching duels, the Red Sox prevailed four games to two.

Grover

In 1920, Grover Cleveland "Pete" Alexander became the second member of the Cubs to perform a pitching Triple Crown with 27 wins, 173 strike-outs, and a 1.91 ERA. The rare feat was nothing new for Grover. He had already won the Triple Crown three times, while pitching for the Philadelphia Phillies. He pitched seven full seasons with the Cubs, but never won a pennant in Chicago.

Pete Alexander won 373 major league games in his career. He ranks third in wins on the all-time list behind Cy Young and Walter Johnson. He was elected to the Hall of Fame in 1938.

Grover Cleveland "Pete" Alexander, Cubs pitcher who won 373 major league games in his career.

Adrian "Cap" Anson played 27 seasons in the big leagues. He began his career with the Cubs in 1876.

Pitcher Grover Cleveland Alexander was elected to the Hall of Fame in 1938.

First baseman Frank Chance, part of the defensive lineup that led the NL in fielding average from 1905-1908.

Mordecai "Three Finger" Brown won 20 or more games for the Cubs every year from 1906-1911.

Cubs

Shortstop Ernie Banks was an NL All-Star 11 times. He joined the Cubs in 1953.

Billy Williams was the NL's Rookie of the Year in 1961.

Ferguson Jenkens began a streak of 6 straight 20-win seasons in 1967.

Center fielder Sammy Sosa finished the 1995 season with 36 home runs and 34 stolen bases.

Wrigley Guarantees It

William Wrigley bought the Cubs in 1921. He promised to use his wealth to bring an NL Pennant back to Chicago. Eventually, he succeeded.

In 1926, Wrigley hired Joe McCarthy to manage the Cubs. He also signed Lewis "Hack" Wilson to play outfield. Hack was 5 feet, 6 inches tall, and stocked with 200 pounds of solid power.

Wrigley traded for outfielder Kiki Cuyler after the 1927 season. In 1929, Rogers Hornsby became the Cubs' second baseman. "Rajah," as Hornsby was known, had won the NL batting crown in seven of the previous nine seasons.

The Cubs won the 1929 NL Pennant by 10.5 games over the Pittsburgh Pirates. Cuyler led the league in stolen bases with 43 for the third time in 4 years. Hornsby and Wilson knocked out 39 homers each, and Hack took his first RBI crown with 159.

The Cubs were beaten in the World Series by Connie Mack's Philadelphia Athletics. Wilson, normally a solid defensive player, took heavy criticism for his blunders in the outfield. McCarthy was also denounced for the World Series loss.

Hack responded in 1930 by setting the NL record for home runs in a season with 56. He also set the major league's all-time RBI record with 190. Hack won the NL home run crown four times in his career. He became a member of the Hall of Fame in 1979.

Rogers Hornsby had a lifetime batting average of .358, second only to Ty Cobb on the major league's all-time list. The "Rajah" was inducted to the Hall of Fame in 1942.

Every Third Year

Chicago's 1929 NL Championship began a quirky streak. The Cubs won an NL Pennant every third year through 1938. With every new title came another World Series defeat.

First baseman Charlie Grimm took over as player-manager midway through the 1932 season. The Cubs won the NL Pennant by four games over the Pittsburgh Pirates. They were led by the pitching of Lon Warneke. In his first full season, Warneke finished on top of the NL with 22 wins, 4 shutouts, and a 2.37 ERA.

Manager Joe McCarthy directed the New York Yankees to a four-game World Series sweep over his former club.

The Cubs won 21 straight games in September, 1935. Grimm managed his second NL Pennant winner. Second baseman Billy Herman batted .341, and led the league in hits, doubles, and fielding average. Chicago was defeated in six games by the Detroit Tigers in the 1935 World Series.

Rogers "Rajah" Hornsby, Cubs' second baseman, fans out in a 1929 World Series loss to the Philadelphia Athletics.

The Streak Ends

The Cubs were in third place halfway through the 1938 season, when Charles "Gabby" Hartnett was named to replace Grimm as player-manager.

Hartnett led all NL catchers in fielding average (.995) for the sixth time in 1938. He and pitcher Charles Root were the only players remaining from the 1929 team that began Chicago's three-year cycle of pennants.

With one week left in the season, the Pittsburgh Pirates came to Wrigley Field leading the Cubs in the NL Pennant race. Jay "Dizzy" Dean pitched for the Cubs in the series opener, and beat the Pirates by a score of 2-1.

The next day, the Cubs rallied for two runs in the eighth inning to tie the score. Gabby Hartnett led-off the bottom of the ninth, after Pittsburgh had gone scoreless in their half of the inning. Hartnett launched a home run that put the Cubs in first place to stay.

The Cubs were swept in the 1938 World Series, again, by the New York Yankees. Their streak of every third pennant ended without a World Championship.

One More Time

Charlie Grimm returned to manage the Cubs in 1944. After five losing seasons, the Cubs were back on top a year later. It was the third time Grimm had led Chicago to a NL Pennant.

First baseman Phil Cavarretta took the 1945 NL batting crown. Hank Wyse led the pitching staff, finishing second in the NL with 22 wins. Ray Prim and Claude Passeau finished first and second in the league in ERA.

Chicago finished three games in front of the St. Louis Cardinals for their sixteenth NL Championship. The Detroit Tigers defeated the Cubs in seven games.

Steve Hack, Cubs' third baseman, is forced out at second base during the fourth and final game of the 1938 World Series against the New York Yankees.

"Let's Play Two!"

Ernie Banks joined the Cubs in 1953. His professional baseball career began with the Kansas City Monarchs of the Negro Leagues. With Chicago, he became one of the greatest power-hitting shortstops of all time.

It was Banks' positive outlook that made him a Chicago legend. He became known to everyone as "Mr. Cub." His love for the game was reflected in his famous remark, "It's a great day for a ballgame. Let's play two!"

Ernie Banks was an NL All-Star 11 times. He was the NL's Most Valuable Player (MVP) in 1958 and 1959. Banks finished with 512 home runs in his 19-year career. He was inducted into the Baseball Hall of Fame in his first year of eligibility, 1977.

Ron Santo came to the Cubs in 1960. He was the NL's Gold Glove third baseman for five straight seasons between 1964-1968.

Playing behind Santo and Banks in left field was Billy Williams. He was the NL's Rookie of the Year in 1961, and was a consistent force in the Cubs' lineup through 1974.

Williams was an All-Star six times, and won the NL's batting crown in 1972. His lifetime production of a .290 batting average, 426 home runs, and 1,475 RBIs, ranks him among the game's greatest players. Billy Williams was inducted into the Hall of Fame in 1987.

Facing page: Shortstop Ernie Banks.

Ferguson Jenkins delivers a pitch enroute to a victory at Wrigley Field against the San Francisco Giants.

Fergie

The Cubs made a trade for a Canadian relief pitcher in 1966. Ferguson Jenkins had just 15 innings of major league experience when he came from the Philadelphia Phillies' bullpen. In Chicago, he became one of the NL's most durable starters.

Jenkins began a streak of 6 straight 20-win seasons in 1967. He led the NL in complete games three times during that period. In 1971, he won the NL's Cy Young Award, after leading the league in wins with 24.

Chicago traded Jenkins to the Texas Rangers in 1974. After eight successful seasons in the AL, Fergie returned to end his career with the Cubs. He retired after the 1983 season with 284 career victories. Ferguson Jenkins became a member of the Hall of Fame in 1991.

Divided We Fall

The NL split into two divisions in 1969. Late in the season, the Cubs looked as if they would take the first NL East Title. But New York's "miracle" season was a disaster for Chicago, as the Mets won the division.

Cub fans waited another 15 years for their team to win a division championship. In 1984, Chicago won the NL East by 6.5 games over the New York Mets. They were led by the NL's MVP, Ryne Sandberg, and the Cy Young Award winner, Rick Sutcliffe.

Ryne Sandberg joined the Cubs in 1982. He became the NL's Gold Glove second baseman the following season. In 1984, Sandberg combined the league's top fielding with some powerful offensive numbers. He won his second of nine straight Gold Glove Awards, as well as the league's MVP honor.

Rick Sutcliffe came to the Cubs in a trade with the Cleveland Indians early in the 1984 season. He won 16 of his 20 starting assignments. Sutcliffe was awarded the league's top pitching honors, while posting an ERA of 2.69.

The Cubs faced the San Diego Padres in the 1984 National League Championship Series. Chicago took a commanding 2-0 lead in the five game series, before dropping three straight games and losing the series.

Andre Dawson came to the Cubs in 1987, after 11 seasons with the Montreal Expos. He led the NL with 49 home runs and 137 RBIs that season, and was named NL MVP. Dawson made his sixth All-Star appearance in 1989. He completed the season with a .310 batting average, the highest of his career.

In 1989, the Cubs finished on top of the NL East again. Mark Grace batted a torrid .647, with 8 RBIs, for the Cubs in the 1989 National League Championship Series. The San Francisco Giants defeated Chicago in five games, and advanced to the World Series.

Generations To Come

The Cubs have thrilled generations of Major League Baseball fans. Hope springs eternal that they will someday return to their World Series glory of 1908. Their current lineup continues to include the Gold Glove of Mark Grace at first base. Sammy Sosa has taken over center field at Wrigley, and finished 1995 with 36 home runs and 34 stolen bases. And Ryne Sandberg has returned after a two-year retirement.

The Cubs may or may not win it all, but one thing is certain: They will continue the legacy of professional baseball in Chicago, and provide the thrill of baseball for generations to come.

Chicago Cubs' slugger Mark Grace watches his broken-bat sacrifice fly during a game against the Pittsburgh Pirates.

Glossary

All-Star: A player who is voted by fans as the best player at one position in a given year.

American League (AL): An association of baseball teams formed in 1900 which make up one-half of the major leagues.

American League Championship Series (ALCS): A best-of-seven-game playoff with the winner going to the World Series to face the National League Champions.

Batting Average: A baseball statistic calculated by dividing a batter's hits by the number of times at bat.

Earned Run Average (ERA): A baseball statistic which calculates the average number of runs a pitcher gives up per nine innings of work.

Fielding Average: A baseball statistic which calculates a fielder's success rate based on the number of chances the fielder has to record an out.

Hall of Fame: A memorial for the greatest baseball players of all time located in Cooperstown, New York.

Home Run (HR): A play in baseball where a batter hits the ball over the outfield fence, scoring everyone on base as well as the batter.

Major Leagues: The highest ranking associations of professional baseball teams in the world, currently consisting of the American and National Baseball Leagues.

Minor Leagues: A system of professional baseball leagues at levels below Major League Baseball.

National League (NL): An association of baseball teams formed in 1876 which make up one-half of the major leagues.

National League Championship Series (NLCS): A best-of-seven-game playoff with the winner going to the World Series to face the American League Champions.

Pennant: A flag which symbolizes the championship of a professional baseball league.

Pitcher: The player on a baseball team who throws the ball for the batter to hit. The pitcher stands on a mound and pitches the ball toward the strike zone area above the plate.

Plate: The place on a baseball field where a player stands to bat. It is used to determine the width of the strike zone. Forming the point of the diamond-shaped field, it is the final goal a base runner must reach to score a run.

RBI: A baseball statistic standing for *runs batted in.* Players receive an RBI for each run that scores on their hits.

Rookie: A first-year player, especially in a professional sport.

Slugging Percentage: A statistic which points out a player's ability to hit for extra bases by taking the number of total bases hit and dividing it by the number of at-bats.

Stolen Base: A play in baseball when a base runner advances to the next base while the pitcher is delivering a pitch.

Strikeout: A play in baseball when a batter is called out for failing to put the ball in play after the pitcher has delivered three strikes.

Triple Crown: A rare accomplishment when a single player finishes a season leading the league in batting average, home runs, and RBIs. A pitcher can win a Triple Crown by leading the league in wins, ERA, and strikeouts.

Walk: A play in baseball when a batter receives four pitches out of the strike zone and is allowed to go to first base.

World Series: The championship of Major League Baseball played since 1903 between the pennant winners from the American and National Leagues.

Index